GIVE YOUR PARENTS A STANDING OVATION!

For Caregivers of Elderly Parents

Dr. Gybrilla Ballard-Blakes

Praise for
Give Your Parents a Standing
Ovation!
by Dr. Gybrilla Ballard-Blakes

Thank you for encouraging us to revere our parents and to honor and cherish every moment. We are so blessed to have them with us.

- Pastor K. Thompson, C.Ed.D.
Remnant of God Deliverance Ministry Inc., Baltimore, MD

I love the title of your new book. It captures the spirit of our ancestors and resonates with the soul of our people.

- Professor Carl O. Snowden
Sojourner Douglass College
Edgewater, MD

GIVE YOUR PARENTS A STANDING OVATION!

For Caregivers of Elderly Parents

Dr. Gybrilla Ballard-Blakes

Dr. Gybrilla Ballard-Blakes

Published by Dr. Gybrilla Blakes
gigiblakes@gmail.com

Scripture quotations are taken from the *Holy Bible, King James Version* (KJV) by Public Domain.

Book design by Dr. Gybrilla Ballard-Blakes
Cover design by Mr. Dorien Minor Sr. and Dr. Karen Thompson
Author photo by Dr. Gybrilla Ballard-Blakes

International Standard Book Number: 978-1499775761
Library of Congress Control Number:

Published in the United States of America

This book is in memory of and dedicated to my parents. I humbly give a standing ovation and thanks to my parents, Edward Ballard Sr. (father) and Elveta Workman Ballard (mother), who were two of the greatest people that I have ever met. Their love, prayers, support, and teachings will always be with me throughout my life. Because of my parents' nurturing and guidance, I know how to rely on God through all of my trials and tribulations. This includes being their caregiver and being able to still stand after their home going.

Contents

Foreword

When we think of the true essence of honoring our parents, as the Lord God has commanded, many adult children who become their parents' caregivers find this command challenging, despite their best intentions. Dr. Gybrilla Blakes has provided a one-of-a kind resource manual to help adult children caregivers deal with these challenges. In this invaluable book, you will learn how to develop appropriate skills to effectively care for your elderly loved ones.

Invaluable resources listed in this book direct you to people, places, programs, and much more in an effort to provide the best daily eldercare possible.

Dr. Blakes is no stranger to being an adult child parental caregiver. The pages of this book are filled with her very own unique experiences and expressions of faith, hope, and love. She understands that this journey is not easy. Hence, in this selfless and tireless labor of love, she reaches out to the world with her gifts. She teaches us how to truly honor our parents throughout the pages of this book.

Give Your Parents a Standing Ovation will encourage and strengthen you. You will cherish this book as a keepsake to pass down through generations, that your days may be prolonged.

Dr. Theriot Shuttlesworth-DuBose
Pastor, Clinical Pastoral Care and Counseling
El Bethel Church, Upper Marlboro, MD

Preface

The purpose of this book is to use my journey as my parents' caregiver to offer support to others walking down a similar path. I also hope to provide resources and survival tools that every caregiver needs.

This is a pious journey that you have embarked upon as a caregiver. In penning this journey, Ephesians 6:2-3 came to mind: "Honour thy father and mother; which is the first commandment with promise; That it may be well with thee, and thou mayest live long on the earth" (King

James Version).

Introduction

"Always give thanks to God, love yourself, and if anything happens to me, please take care of your mother."

As a child, I heard this saying quite often, and throughout my life, I have tried to follow my father's directive. I wrote this book to use my journey as my parents' caregiver to support others in their own journey. Indeed, it is one of the most personal things I have to share, in hopes that it contains some universal value others might find helpful. My journey as a caregiver began when my father was in his late sixties and my mother in her early sixties. Later, when my father died and my mother was eighty-two years old, I assumed full-time responsibility as her caregiver until she passed away at age eighty-four.

The contents of this book were derived from a saying that my parents would often use when I was struggling with a difficult situation: "This too will pass, so don't think that you are the first or the only person who has gone through this. 'For with God nothing shall be impossible' (Luke 1:37, King James Version)."

This piece of wisdom has gotten me through some really thorny times in my life. Wisdom like this is the reason it is imperative for me to write about my journey, so that it might lighten the burden of someone else's journey. It is the underlying meaning of that wisdom that has always intrigued me. My spiritual foundation was laid early in my childhood.

"Always give thanks to God. Love yourself; and if anything happens to me, please take care of your mother."

This too will pass, and with God, you will survive whatever you are going through. These types of affirmations are what give me strength to hold my head up day by day. Because my parents were so instrumental in the development of my Christian beliefs and introduced me to most of these affirmations, I titled this book *Give Your Parents a Standing Ovation.*

Chapter 1

Mentors

When I am asked whether I had a mentor or who my mentor was, I am proud to say that my parents were my mentors. My parents were two exceptional people. I say this because they never appeared to get tired of answering questions, explaining, or clarifying issues for me. My parents were married for over sixty years and instilled in their children the importance of being a supportive family. Our home was the house where all the neighborhood kids and their parents wanted to visit. My parents were highly respected in the community. Church, school, and neighborhood families often came to them for advice and guidance . I could go to my parents for guidance with any problem or concern. My parents were always my springboard or shoulders to lean on. Their support is the second reason I have evolved into the person I am today. Of course, the first is Almighty God.

Dr. Gybrilla Ballard-Blakes

From the time I was a child, I would sit with my parents for hours, listening and asking questions about all kinds of things. Some people commented that I hung around my parents too much. But I never cared what other people said about our relationship, because the wisdom I gained from my parents is priceless. Every day, I rely

on the wisdom I received from them,
which keeps me from fretting
needlessly or making a lot of useless
mistakes.

> **"Every day, I rely on the wisdom I received from my parents, which keeps me from fretting or making a lot of useless mistakes."**

Both of my parents expressed to me how important it is to do the right thing; therefore, when I am confronted with a problem, it is easier for me to resolve it. I remember when I was a college student working on a summer job. Before the fall term started, my supervisor offered me a new permanent position with a better salary. However, the drawback was that if I accepted the new position, I would have to quit school. When I shared the new job offer with my parents, they were unhappy.

They could not believe that I would consider taking the job and quitting school. As I look back, I realize that is where my career and education could have taken a different turn had I not had supportive parents whose opinions I dearly respected. I was young and I did not have a clue that taking a permanent job without a degree could have drastically changed my education and career path.

Making the right choice was another life lesson my parents taught me at an early age. They would tell me, "The choices you make today will dictate future outcomes." As a child, this made no sense; however, as I continued to make both good and bad choices and experiencing the

> *"My parents were always my springboard or shoulders to lean on."*

outcomes, it became clearer to me. This continued into adulthood. At one point, I was confronted with a major life-changing decision of maintaining my existing retirement plan or changing to a new one. As always, I discussed my options with my parents.

At the time, I was only two years into the old retirement plan, so when my job started offering gifts and advertising how wonderful the new retirement plan was, I was tempted to switch. I saw several of my colleagues switching and receiving gifts, but I was not fully convinced. I recall my father asked me this question: "Why would your agency give gifts and continue to push or advertise a new retirement plan in this fashion if it was truly better than the one that you already have?" The differences between the two retirement plans were initially very confusing; however, as time went on, it became clear that my agency was giving the employees all of the pros and none of the cons of the new retirement plan. Well, thank God I did not switch to the new plan, because, as usual, my mentors were right with their assessment and guidance. Had I given into the advertising gimmicks, I would have lost, at a minimum, 50 percent of my annual retirement salary.

Now when I am faced with a decision that causes me to pause, my mind automatically goes to my parents, because all of my life, I have relied on them to provide guidance and serve as a barometer. It is amazing that you don't realize how much you rely on someone until they are no longer there. I was really blessed to have had my parents/mentors because they not only gave me wisdom, they also gave me a solid life foundation that has prepared and allowed me to deal with the many bumps in the road that everyday life brings. All the guidance and wisdom I received from my parents, throughout my life, has enabled me to have strength when I am weak and to know where true strength comes from. "I can do all things through Christ which strengtheneth me" (Philippians 4:13, King James Version). So when it was my turn to become a caregiver for my parents, this Bible verse is what I reflected on to give me strength when I felt weak.

_____

Chapter 2

When It Is Your Turn: Your Elderly Parent and You

As adults, we often reflect upon our childhood, when we were taken care of by our parents. Our parents took us to school and to doctor's appointments, drove us where we needed to go, took care of us when we were sick or gave us medicine, fixed our meals, washed our clothes, etc. In many families, the parent and child roles will switch from the parent taking care of their children to the adult child becoming a caregiver for their elderly parent.

When a parent and their child switch roles, it can create challenges in the relationship, because the child becomes the leader or caregiver. Some children who become caregivers for their parents begin to believe that since they have switched roles, now it is their turn to be the parent. Switching roles from the child into the parental caregiver can cause some confusion as to who has to listen to whom. The confusion comes because the child is now taking the parent to their doctor's appointments, giving baths, assisting them with putting on clothing, washing their clothes, fixing meals, driving them around, administering medicine, etc. However, although roles may switch, one thing that you should always remember is that you are still the child and your parents are still your parents!

It is fair to say that your childhood

relationship with your parents can be

an advantage or disadvantage when

you are their caregiver. For example, if

your relationship was good and you respected your parents as a child, when roles switch, you will more than likely try to be a good and supportive caregiver. However, if your relationship was difficult or you had little contact with your parents as a child, when roles switch, you will more than likely find caregiving to be burdensome or challenging. Nevertheless, you have been placed in this role because your parents are no longer able to independently handle some or all daily tasks or personal affairs.

To help parents maintain some of

their independence, caregivers should allow them to continue to handle any of their personal business that they are still able to handle.

It was sometime in the late 1990s that I noticed that my parents began to show signs of aging. Specifically, I noticed their aging:

> When I assumed more responsibility for my parents' banking;
> When my father needed me to wash his trucks and cars for him;
> When my father fell asleep while cooking dinner once;
> When my parents needed assistance threading a needle;
> When my father finally started using a cane or scooter to get around;

➢ When my parents reduced their number of road trips;
➢ When my parents decided to permanently move into their one-level home;
➢ When my parents had a taller commode installed in the house;
➢ When my mother started to worry when going down the steps;
➢ When my father more frequently requested me to take care of my mother if he were to leave first; and
➢ When my mother would misplace things.

They started relying on me to help them with the personal things that they used to do on their own. But I found that allowing my parents to make their own decisions on everything possible made life easier for us all. I never forgot that I was their child and my role was to support my parents and ensure that their wishes were met and their well-being enhanced.

> *"I never forgot that I was their child. My role was to support my parents and ensure that their wishes were met and their well-being enhanced."*

A caregiver's personal responsibilities can sometimes affect their effectiveness when caring for an elderly parent. Therefore, when roles switch and you become a caregiver for your elderly parent, you must be mindful to do your best to balance your caregiver responsibilities and your personal responsibilities.

Caring for my parents was a rewarding experience. I thank God for giving me an opportunity to give back to my aging parents. Now, I would be remiss not to say that with the rewards and joy I got from this, there were also challenges, stress, and frustration.

Understanding what's involved in caring for a parent means understanding more deeply the relationship between parents and their children, as well as their obligations and responsibilities. While you may not be able to physically care for your parent due to a number of circumstances, there are things that you can do to foster their independence, enhance their quality of life, and create even stronger parent-child bonds. In this book, you will find resources to support your parents, as well as yourself, the caregiver.

Chapter 3

Your Turn, Your Role: Tips for Parent Caregivers

Tip 1: Stay Positive

I always

remembered

that just

**TIP 1
"Try to stay positive when your parent is being stubborn."**
___

because my parents may have needed some emotional or physical support during their later stages of life, this did not mean that I had a right to treat them like children. I treated my aging parents like they were my parents. Caregivers should treat their parents or other elders with respect; they should try to stay positive when their parent is being stubborn about things, such as not wanting to eat, dodging a doctor's appointment, or refusing to take a bath. I found that being positive when my parents were reluctant to do something often led to them changing their mind. I would agree with their decision, unless it could have caused them harm. I think my parents allowed me to make a lot of decisions for them because I always assured them that as their child, I respected whatever they said and had their best interest at heart. Sometimes it can be difficult, but caregivers can do it. If you let your parent or your elderly loved one know that they still have some control over their lives, you will be surprised at how much they will try to do. Losing the respect of children and other loved ones due to weakness, handicap, or disease can be devastating to the elderly. It affects more their physical health; it also affects their emotional state.

I witnessed this firsthand when I was my mom's caregiver.

Tip 2: Include Them in Decisions

I always kept my parents involved in their financial and healthcare decisions. Even if the parents can't take care of such issues on their own, caregivers should make every effort to include their parents in decisions concerning their own lives. I included my parents in the process on everything that involved them as often as possible and for as long as possible. Caregivers should do their best to respect their parents' wishes regarding their finances and healthcare, and involve them in any important decision-making processes, such as home healthcare, long-term nursing care, powers-of-attorney documents, and end-of-life wishes.

> **TIP 2**
> **"Make every effort to include your parents."**

As a caregiver, you should try to reassure your parents, regardless of their physical, mental, and emotional state, and make every effort

to have continuous communication.
Take the initiative and assume that
your parent can understand you. Take
the time to explain what's happening,
and reassure your parents that you're
doing what you can to
abide by their wishes.

Tip 3: Help Them Maintain Dignity

If you are a parental
caregiver, please
remember the elder is
an adult and has
experienced life. Don't

talk down to them, boss them around,
nag them about habits, or dictate to

45

them how they should behave. Research has shown that some medications and certain medical conditions, such as different types of dementia (like Alzheimer's disease), may alter your parent's personality or attitude, but caregivers must do their best not to treat the parent like a child who doesn't know any better. Aging parents struggle to maintain their dignity. Consequently, as their caregiver, you should avoid discussing your parents' personal affairs with another person while your parents are in the room. Treating your parents as though they are invisible, deaf, or uncomprehending is not the best way to preserve their dignity.

Tip 4: The Golden Rule

The bottom line is, caregivers should remember that they are the child caring for an elderly parent, and in the future, they may also need a caregiver. Therefore, as caregivers, we should treat our parents in the same fashion that we would like to be treated, regardless of physical or mental limitations. Some

TIP 4
"Your parent is a human being that deserves to be treated with respect, compassion, and dignity, regardless of their circumstances."

elderly parents are afraid. They may be uneasy with their state of being or the fact that they are losing some or most of their independence. Many caregivers have found that their parents are hesitant to rely on loved ones or the charity of others for their well-being. First and foremost, caregivers must remember that their parent is a human being and deserves to be treated with respect, compassion, and dignity, regardless of their circumstances. As a caregiver, you also need to remember that your parent has gone through life, experienced a variety of emotions, and may even have struggled and suffered.

Chapter 4

Living Far Away from Elderly Parents

My parents were in their late seventies and early eighties, living in Sumter, South Carolina. I lived and remain in

"I called my parents several times a day to just talk and to make sure"

Bowie, Maryland. As one of twelve siblings, I have five older sisters, four older brothers, and two younger brothers. We were all in our thirties, forties, and fifties at the time our parents needed caregiving, and none of us lived in South Carolina. In fact, most of us lived in Maryland or Virginia. Although all of us visited our parents, only I and two of my brothers visited regularly.

My family did not have a set schedule for visiting our parents. However, I assumed personal responsibility in making sure our parents had all the support they needed. None of my siblings dictated when or which sibling would visit our parents.

Although the majority of time it was my two brothers or me visiting our parents, we never argued or complained about our other siblings not helping our parents or visiting them. I called my parents several times a day to just talk and to make sure they were OK. Sometimes, I would sit on the phone with my parents for long periods of time, trying to help them find a channel on their cable TV or assisting them with setting up a new cellular phone, etc.

It did not matter that we had other

family who lived near our parents in South Carolina; I still assumed responsibility for taking care of my parents' personal needs. For years, I took both of my parents to all of their doctor's appointments.

During my visits with my parents, I would go shopping and stock up on enough food and personal items to last them until my next visit. Often, I would stay with my aging parents for two weeks or more.

For many years in their old age, my parents continued to maintain their household and a pond surrounded by fifty acres with livestock. It was a very stressful time for me, because my parents, like most aging adults, wanted to be independent.

I knew that since it was important to my parents to maintain their independence, I needed to support their wishes as much as possible. Having long-distance elderly parents was stressful at times, because my siblings and I had full-time jobs, businesses, families, and other life responsibilities too. Although I knew I had to leave it in God's hands, it was a horrible and sickening feeling each time I had to leave my elderly parents to go back home. It was sad and hard to leave my parents, because I knew that they really needed me to assist them every day, so I felt guilty, stressed, and unhappy

> "Having long-distance elderly parents was stressful at times, because my siblings and I had full-time jobs, businesses, families, and other life responsibilities too."

Dr. Gybrilla Ballard-Blakes

when I left them.

Chapter 5

What About Me?

Feelings of Stress, Hopelessness, Guilt

In some ways, being a caregiver is similar to following airline safety instructions: put on your oxygen mask before helping someone else put on theirs. Balancing caregiving with other areas of my life was challenging. While I was my parents' caregiver, I was working a full-time job, teaching graduate school part-time, completing a PhD program, and was also a wife. In 2007, after my dad passed away, my mom came to live with me, so I adjusted my schedule to ensure that I spent quality time with her. I was under unbelievable stress and pressure, because it seemed there was never enough time in a day to complete everything that I had to do. There were so many days that I felt guilty about not being able to spend time with my mom because I had to go to work, complete a homework assignment, or just did not balance my time appropriately. When I think about all of the things I was involved in during the time I was a caregiver, I praise God for His mercy and grace that got me through it. So how can you get through the stress and clashing demands? Here are some tips from the American Association of Retired Persons (AARP) to *keep your stress in check:*

1. Put your physical needs first
2. Stay connected with friends
3. Ask for help
4. Call on community resources
5. Take a break
6. Deal with your feelings
7. Find time to relax
8. Get organized

9. Just say no

10. Stay positive

My mom always had a pretty healthy appetite (fresh fruits and vegetables, salads, fish, and beans), so I was able to share nutritious meals with her. I kept my stress-driven urges to a minimum by praying, meditating, and working out as often as possible. My daughter or my mom's hired caregiver helped me with my mom when I worked out. I did not have time to go to a fitness center, but I had workout equipment in my basement. Therefore, I ran on the treadmill, lifted weights, got in the sauna, and used other types of workout equipment at home. I have always gotten a medical physical every year, but when I was my mom's caregiver, I made sure that I paid even closer attention to my health. I wanted to stay healthy so I could focus on taking care of her.

When I was my mom's caregiver, I spent most of my time with her and very little with friends and relatives.

My mom and I went to the park/pond on most nice days when I got home from work. We went shopping often, and we went out to eat at a restaurant every Friday night, so that Mom could have something to look forward to every weekend.

Since I spent the majority of my free time with my mom only, when she passed away, I was traumatized and depressed for months. I would recommend that caregivers not isolate themselves from other family members and friends while they are caring for their parents, even if they feel guilty about leaving or not spending enough time with their parents. I recommend this because I don't think it would have been as devastating for me if I had spent a little more time doing other things.

I felt guilty every time I left my mom, but I knew I had to continue handling my own personal business. Therefore, when I was my mom's caregiver, I had no problem asking for help, because I quickly understood that if I did not ask for help, I would cause myself unnecessary stress. However, I was very particular when choosing who I would ask because my mom would tell me when she was not comfortable with certain people. So most of the time, I asked my daughter Ginnifer, my brother and his wife, or the lady who kept my mom during the day when I went to work. Fortunately, I had my twenty-one-year-old daughter, my husband, and a few friends I could rely on to share my feelings or to just vent about things I was dealing with. I think when you are a caregiver, a way to minimize your stress and anxiety is to have some form of nonalcoholic, nondrug stress reliever and/or communication outlet. The reason I think caregivers should have an outlet is that it gives them a venue to relieve what they are experiencing.

This communication outlet could be a person, a support group, an employment work-life program, a family member, or a friend who is or has been a caregiver for the elderly.

For years, I practiced relaxation

methods, and when I was my mom's caregiver, this really helped me get through some tough times. I also sat in the sauna in my basement for fifteen to thirty minutes as often as possible.

I used a calendar and a to-do-list for all of my and my mom's appointments and other activities. This really helped me keep track of all of my mom's doctors and other appointments, meals, and any other important events. I also kept good records of my mom's bills and financial records. I used an electronic calendar and my mom's bank's electronic bill-pay for keeping track of and paying bills.

As my mom's caregiver, I had no problem saying no when I was asked to take on another project or financial obligation, because as most caregivers for the elderly will confirm, my hands were full taking care of my mom. For example, I did not travel as much for my full-time job, and I decreased the number of classes I taught at my university.

Relaxation methods, such as deep breathing, prayer, and meditation, help place you in a positive state of mind. Therefore, I would recommend these methods to all caregivers if you find yourself in a negative state or if you are having a conflict with your siblings or other relatives. As a caregiver and during other stressful periods in my life, I have experienced firsthand that prayer and meditation resolve all negative feelings. In the morning and before I went to sleep every night I routinely prayed and listened to stress-relieving music and meditation apps on my iPad.

Chapter 6

It Doesn't Matter Matter What Your Mask Is: *As a Caregiver, You Must Put Your Mask on First*

The most important and number one thing that most caregivers neglect to do is to take care of themselves. If you have ever flown in an airplane, one of the first warnings you hear from the flight attendant is you most put your oxygen mask on first before helping someone else. Your first thought was probably, *Well that would be selfish to save myself first and then help my mom, dad, child, or someone else.* Most caregivers have this same mindset when it comes to caring for their parents, a patient, or an elderly person. However, the same principle applies to caregivers: if you do not take care of yourself first, you will not be able to effectively take care of the people you love. Most caregivers have a tendency to do for others, because they are naturally nurturing, caring, supportive, loving, and responsible people.

Please remember, you're not being selfish in taking time for you; actually, you are being proactive and responsible, especially if your goal is to be an effective caregiver. By putting on your mask first, you are putting yourself in an utmost position to handle all of the day-to-day responsibilities that comes with being a caregiver. Your caregiver's responsibilities are huge, but taking care of yourself first is a very important ingredient in becoming a successful caregiver and maintaining your health. Therefore, if you place your mask on first, this will increase your chances of helping your loved ones.

According to AgingCare.com (2013), rough statistics show that 30 percent of caregivers die before those they are caring for. Some studies show death rates higher—as much as 35 to 40 percent. Illness that doesn't lead to death is rampant, and depression and auto-immune diseases are high on the list.

Stanford University's study on caregiving for patients with Alzheimer's disease (2012) states, "For Alzheimer's and dementia patients, caregiving responsibilities can last between 10 and 15 years. During that time, caregivers often experience mental health problems such as depression, anxiety and substance abuse, along with physical health problems. Researchers have discovered that Alzheimer's caregivers have a 63 percent higher mortality rate than non-caregivers (especially if the caregivers are between 66-96 years old). In fact, 40 percent of

Dr. Gybrilla Ballard-Blakes

Alzheimer's caregivers die from stress-related disorders before the patient dies."

As my mom's caregiver, I was very mindful to take care of myself, by exercising, meditating, listening to inspirational music, getting proper sleep, taking time to relax, getting regular medical check-ups, and, most of all, praying. I knew that my responsibilities as a caregiver were very stressful at times; therefore, I kept a list of known stress symptoms as a reminder. I reviewed this list often just in case I needed to contact a counselor, psychologist, or other mental health professional for help, due to the following stress symptoms:

- ✓ Becoming easily irritated or angered
- ✓ Frequent headaches, bodily pain, or other physical problems
- ✓ Sleeping too much or too little
- ✓ Feeling tired most of the time
- ✓ Loss of interest in activities you used to enjoy
- ✓ Feeling constantly worried
- ✓ Often feeling sad
- ✓ Gaining or losing a lot of weight
- ✓ Abuse of alcohol, illegal drugs or prescription drugs

✓ Feeling overwhelmed or unable to cope

When I was my mom's caregiver, I went through a lot of challenges, and trial and error, because I did not know that there were caregiver support groups and tons of other resources for caregivers on the Web to help you maintain your mind, body, and soul. Caregivers should surf the Web for supportive tips and resources to help them on their journey. However, caregivers should also remember: it does not matter what your mask is, *you must put your mask on first!*

Chapter 7

Legal
Responsibility
Get Power of Attorney

What is a Power of Attorney (POA)?

Power of attorney (POA) is normally given to a loved one, trusted friend, or attorney to legally handle the principal's personal affairs.

POA is a written document that gives someone the legal right to act (or make decisions) on behalf of someone else concerning finances, private affairs, business, healthcare, and other legal matters.

The person who gives the rights (your elderly parent, in this case) is called the "principal."

The person given the rights (you, in this case) is called the "agent." The principal can change or void this POA at any time. The POA is terminated when the principal dies.

There are several types of POAs, including conventional and durable. This is why it is imperative for your loved one to consult with an attorney who is familiar with

> *POA is a written document that gives someone the legal right to act (or make decisions) on behalf of someone else concerning finances, private affairs, business, healthcare, and other legal matters.*

POAs, because when an agent is appointed, they can act on the principal's behalf only under certain circumstances.

A POA gives the designated agent permission to act on the principal's behalf if they become incapacitated.

If the principal designates a person they can trust, it gives them assurance that their finances and, if applicable, their healthcare will be handled in their best interest. A power of attorney also gives the principal comfort because it can be voided at any time.

Types of POAs

A *conventional* power of attorney gives the agent the authority to act on the principal's behalf.

The conventional POA begins when it is signed and usually ends when or if the principal becomes mentally incompetent. A principal can assign conventional POAs for very specific reasons/periods of time (handle finances from x date to y date) or for general reasons (i.e., handle all finances). You must add a specific note in the conventional P O A if the principal wants someone to make decisions for them beyond the point at which they become mentally incompetent. A *springing* power of attorney gives the agents the authority to act on behalf of the principal if there is some unforeseen event that causes the principal to become incompetent.

However, under this POA, the principal can still handle their own personal affairs until they become incapacitated. This type of POA remains valid until it is canceled by the principal or until the principal passes away.

My sister and I jointly held a *durable* power of attorney for our mom. I was the primary agent and my sister was the substitute agent. We didn't have any conflicts with this arrangement until my mom got really sick. Then, oh my God! I have heard of sibling relationships that changed when a parent got sick or died, but I was totally taken aback by the challenges and conflicts I faced with my sister.

Our relationship took a 180 degree turn for the worse in the months before and after our mom passed away. I was shocked since my siblings and I usually got along reasonably well, especially when it came to our parents. Although I had been taking care of the majority of my parents' personal affairs, bills, and finances for years, some of my siblings did not think I should have been chosen to be my mom's primary agent. So I will caution any sibling, family member, or friend who becomes a primary agent or substitute agent for the principal to make sure they keep good records and be prepared to answer any questions or concerns from other family members or legal entities. As the primary agent for my mom, I found it very stressful dealing with my siblings, but I got through it by focusing on what our mom's needs were and doing a lot of praying. Accepting the role of a primary agent can cause you to become estranged from your siblings and other family members. However, remember that your goal is to take care of your parents and focus on what's best for them! *Powers of attorneys are invalid and the authority of the agent expires once the principal dies.*

Choosing an Agent

When or if your aging parent decides to choose an agent for their power of attorney, they should ensure that they can trust the person they choose and that this person is able and willing to handle this very important responsibility. Your parent should consult with an attorney to prepare the POA, so that they can make sure that it has all legal rights included. They can pick a family member, a close friend, or their attorney to act as an agent. What is most important for your parent to remember when choosing an agent is that this person has access to the principal's finances and can make withdrawals, although these withdrawals must only be made on behalf of the principals.

As stated earlier, a power of attorney is automatically null and void immediately after the principal's death.

When I became my mom's primary agent, I ensured that I included her in everything I did on her behalf until she passed away. I also kept extremely good records on everything I did under the authority of the POA. Because I kept good records, I was able to answer the questions posed later by my siblings and the courts.

Chapter 8

Progression of Elderly Parents

Changes in Lifestyle

At some point in your caregiving journey, you may need a professional partner, such as a nursing home, assisted living, home health, hospice, or adult daycare. When considering care providers, you need to weigh the options and ask the right questions to ensure that both you and your loved one are comfortable with whatever arrangements you make. If at all possible, caregivers should include their parents in choosing a home healthcare provider.

According to Healy et al. (2012), 43 million Americans provide care for someone older than fifty who has age-related issues or is disabled, including 15 million who care for someone with Alzheimer's disease or dementia. Nearly one in ten women ages forty-five to fifty-six is a member of the "sandwich generation, taking care of an aging parent and her own children at the same time, according to a report from the Department of Labor" (Healy, 2012). There may come a point when trying to convince your parent about the realities of their health and living situation won't be effective. There is an approach called "validation therapy," where you focus on validating what your parent is feeling. You can say, "Mom, I know you'd really want to live in your own house and I understand why." It often works to change the subject and bring it around to something she's more comfortable with. Although my mom never got to the later stages of dementia, some caregivers have to put their parents into a nursing home because they can no longer take care of them at home.

You can receive Family Medical Leave Act (FMLA) job protection as a caregiver for a parent. See what home care programs your aging parent may be eligible for, talk to your local aging office (eldercare.gov), or call AARP. Sometimes home-based services are also offered on a sliding-fee scale based on what your loved one can afford, so be sure to ask about that. Also connect with other caregivers in your online community.

Home Care

When my dad passed away, my siblings and I had to ensure that our mom was taken care of. We knew that the only options we had were to allow our mom to stay in her own home or for her to come and live with one of us. Our dad was adamant that if anything happened to him, he wanted me and my siblings to take care of our mom, and he asked us not to put our mom into a nursing home.

So I volunteered to take our mom home to live with me, if she was willing. Mom agreed. When she moved in with us, we chose a home health partner to help take care of her until she passed away.

Mom and I chose a caregiver we had known for several years. I looked into home healthcare agencies, but I wasn't motivated enough to conduct any interviews.

Also, I didn't want to ask my mom if she would consider speaking with the agency caregivers, because we had been through that process with my dad before he passed away. Unfortunately, we had a bad experience. I recommend you research and make your selection wisely if you choose this route. Here are some of the problems we ran into in utilizing agency home healthcare for my dad:

- ✓ Some of the caregivers lacked training in some of their agency's listed care

- ✓ Caregivers arriving late for work

- ✓ Inadequate care to patients

- ✓ Replacement of caregiver employees regularly

✓ Poor record-keeping
by caregivers on care
provided

While working with healthcare agencies didn't work for me, I understand it may be a good option for others. It's a good idea to check in, monitor, and keep up with each person who is going into your loved one's home on a regular basis. There are several websites with more specific information on hiring a home care worker and tips for managing stress to help you hang in there. To find out what your parent is eligible for, visit the AARP website (www.aarp.org).

My mom and I felt very comfortable with the family friend we hired to be her home caregiver. We were so impressed, in fact, that when my mom needed a twenty-four-hour caregiver, this person was the only caregiver we used or even considered. We were blessed to have a caregiver that we trusted and who did a fantastic job of caring for my mom. If you and your parent trust and feel comfortable with your parent's caregiver, it can really ease stress and anxiety for both of you.

Dr. Gybrilla Ballard-Blakes

Assisted Living Facilities assist people of all ages that need daily monitoring of their living and healthcare activities due to a health issue or aging. This type of facility provides nurses, rehabilitation services, healthcare providers, and any other type of help needed to assist in support of ill patients.

Adult Daycare provides daily supervised activities, day trips, small meals, and a place for elderly and handicapped people to socialize and have interaction with other people during the day. These facilities normally have free and/or paid transportation to and from the participant's residence.

In our case, my mom was so impressed with her home caregiver that she did not want to go to an adult daycare. The great thing about adult daycare centers is the fact that most states have free transportation for seniors, so we did have that option, had we chosen to utilize it. While I never utilized the adult daycare for my mom, it was comforting to have this option available.

Nursing Homes are facilities for the elderly and seriously ill people that need assistance with their medical and personal care. Seniors sometimes go to nursing homes when they are no longer able to take care of themselves independently.

Before I started writing this book, I did not know that there were websites with excellent resources to help caregivers take care of their parents. I relied on the Veteran's Administration only. There is a list of resources for nursing homes at the medicare.gov website. You can view all the nursing homes in your area and compare them on their quality measures, such as controlling pain and even bedsores. Most important, be sure the agency is certified and licensed, and the workers bonded. This website also has a point-of-contact list for every community that has a person who monitors and addresses issues in nursing homes. That's the long-term care ombudsman. To find the ombudsman or support groups in your area, go to eldercare.gov. You might also find a local geriatric care manager or assisted-living locator service (they usually do nursing homes too) in your area to have someone show you local options

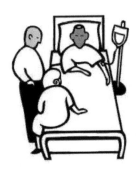

Hospice is care provided for patients who are in the last stages of life. This care is normally provided when medical doctors have exhausted their treatment options for a patient. Hospice care can be provided in a terminally ill person's home, a hospital, or a nursing home. My mom

was never considered terminally ill; therefore, she did not need hospice care.

Chapter 9

Caregiver Toolkit

If you're a caregiver, part of your job may be to keep track of your loved one's legal affairs. This can be a serious challenge for most caregivers, because you are responsible for protecting yourself as well as your elderly family member's legal planning.

The AARP (2013) advises that the ultimate goal is to make sure you have all the decision-making rights you need to manage your loved one's affairs.

Cosmato and Scheid (2011) offer six tips on how to protect your relative's legal rights—and your own. I have also added a couple of additional items you may find useful.

1: Have the right documents

In addition to a **will,** make sure your loved one has a **healthcare power of attorney (POA)** as well as a power of attorney for financial decisions. These legal documents will allow an appointed person to make decisions

for a frail or incapacitated relative.

2: Legal guidance

(http://www.brighthub.com/money/pers

onal- finance/articles/70944.aspx)

- How to manage someone else's money

- How to write an ethical will

- How to appeal denied insurance claims

Your loved one needs to create these

documents when he or she is still

capable of making decisions. It's not

necessary to hire an attorney to draft a

healthcare POA (though depending

on your state, you may need two witnesses). But it's best to use a lawyer to draw up a financial power of attorney, because money issues can be complicated.

The healthcare POA should spell out your loved one's wishes, such as when life-sustaining treatment should be stopped (also known as a living will). You can find free advance directive forms and instructions on what to do in your state on the AARP website. Also, the American Bar Association's website has a toolkit for healthcare planning.

3: Make a family plan

Discuss caregiving matters with all involved members of your family. Have your loved one put in writing who will be responsible for which caregiving roles, and have all parties sign. This is not a legal document, but it will help keep peace within the family by making everyone's role clear. Bad communication can be one of the biggest causes of legal problems.

4: Organize important papers

Most people don't realize how many legal documents they already have, or how many they will need for matters that arise. Important ones include birth and marriage certificates, divorce decrees, citizenship papers, death certificate of a spouse or parent, power of attorney, deeds to property and cemetery plots, veteran's discharge papers, insurance policies, and pension benefits. Organize these documents into files that are easy to navigate.

5: Explore potential financial help

Investigate public benefits, such as Social Security and Supplemental Security Income (SSI) disability programs, veterans' benefits, Supplemental Nutrition Assistance Program (SNAP, formerly known as Food Stamps), Medicare, and Medicaid. The AARP Foundation offers an online tool, Benefits QuickLINK, to help determine if your loved one qualifies for fifteen different government programs. The National Council on Aging offers a similar online tool called Benefits Checkup.

Also, examine your loved one's private disability or life insurance coverage, their pension benefits, their long-term care insurance, and their employee health insurance policy, to see whether any of them cover home health visits, skilled nursing, physical therapy, or any kind of short-term assistance, which could include a mental health therapist or physical therapy. If you take a leave of absence from your job to care for a loved one, you are entitled to three months of unpaid leave from your employer under the Family and Medical Leave Act (FMLA) and are guaranteed your job when you return.

6: Think beyond your loved one

If your parent is unable to take care of people who depended on him or her, you may need to assume or assign that role. This includes assuming responsibility for adult children with special needs. Make such children get every available benefit, such as Social Security disability, local and state disability, special education programs, and free transportation for the disabled. You may also need to assume oversight of benefits of the surviving spouse as well, by making sure the spouse is the beneficiary of your loved one's IRA, bank account, life insurance policy, and pension benefits. Your loved one may also have a plan for pets in the will, and money set aside to pay for their care.

7: Look for tax breaks and life insurance deals

Keep all medical expense receipts for tax deductions. Your family member may claim federal deductions for many medical expenses, including a hospital bed or wheelchair, out-of-pocket expenses not covered by health insurance (drug costs and copayments), remodeling the home to make it handicapped accessible, and a respite caregiver to give the main caregiver a break.

Also, find out whether your family member has a life insurance policy that makes accelerated death payments to help pay for long-term care.

8: Planning for the funeral

My parents talked to me about their advance directives, funeral plans, and the like. Your parent's final wishes are such an important issue and such an important family conversation—and such a difficult one. If you let your parents know how worried you are that something might happen to them before they have told you what their wishes are, they may be more willing to provide the information. I told my parents how much I loved them, and how much I wanted the best for them, and that I wanted the peace of mind of knowing that I honored their final wishes.

Chapter 10

You Are Not Alone with the Diagnosis of Dementia

Early in the year 2000, my mom went to the hospital because she wasn't feeling well. Upon taking the medicine prescribed during the visit, she hallucinated for about eight hours.

This concerned our family for a while, but my mom's hallucinations went away with what we thought was no trace.

By the middle of the year 2000, my dad would ask my mom why she did not pay a bill when the money was in the bank, and she couldn't remember. He would ask her where she placed something, and again, she couldn't remember. Although my mom would go ahead and pay the bill or eventually find what she was looking for, these events began to happen more often.

While our family thought that my mom's hallucinations were a one-time problem that was triggered by doctors giving her the wrong medicine, we later realized her forgetfulness was occurring more often. My parents asked me to set up a doctor's appointment for my mom to have her checked out, because she and my dad began to notice that she could not remember things as well as she once could. I set up several doctor's appointments with a well-known neuropharmacologist. After careful evaluation of my mom, the neuropharmacologist diagnosed her with the first stage of dementia. My mom's was devastating to my family, because we felt that there were no answers to our thousand questions. My mom was a true matriarch for our family, so when we got the bad news that she was in the first stage of dementia, we felt totally lost. Actually, my family was in a funk for several months as we dealt with the realization that our mom would more than likely lose her memory and possibly become very ill.

Surprisingly, our mom did not show further signs of dementia for years. It seemed as though she started to visibly show signs of dementia after the deaths of several of her family members and some other stressful situations in her life. Even after she started to show signs, like becoming confused in the evenings or not being able to remember certain things, she was always able to recognize all of her family members (husband, children, siblings, etc.) until she passed away. By the grace of the Almighty God, my mom was able to continue to have meaningful conversations, give parental advice, and answer her doctor's questions until a month before she passed away. I believe that because we continued to communicate with my mom, she was able to continue to communicate effectively, even with dementia.

Most people who have a family member with dementia wonder why their family member has to go through such a horrible illness. The *2012 Alzheimer's Disease Facts and Figures* offers statistics showing that over 5.4 million people in the United States suffer from Alzheimer's, the most common type of dementia. Alzheimer's destroys brain cells and causes confusion, anger, mood swings, language breakdown, and long-term memory loss.

Your aging family member's doctor can help you find the right resources and community to help you with this challenging diagnosis. Any given facility can tell you what structured activities are available, whether there are secured areas to prevent wandering, common symptom of the disease, and other important details—all without cost or obligation to you.

24/7 Care for a Parent Who Has Dementia

If you are a caregiver for a parent with any of the seven stages of dementia, you may be having a difficult time finding a balance between work, home, and caring for your parent. You may find yourself getting uptight more quickly, spending time alone, and feeling like there is not enough time to spend with the rest of the family. Getting frustrated with a parent who shows symptoms of dementia or who has been diagnosed with dementia is not helpful for anyone; however, I still found myself getting sucked into that trap. I was blessed that my parents had the option of staying in their own home or staying with one of my siblings or me until they passed away. However, I would advise caregivers transitioning their parents to anywhere outside of their home to try to maintain familiar routines. The more you can get them into the new routines but keep elements of the old, the better your parents will transition.

I moved my mom from South Carolina to Maryland after my dad passed away. My siblings and I made the decision to move our mom to Maryland because most of us lived there and we wanted to ensure that she was close to most of her children. Also, I did not want to continue to be a long-distance caregiver. It's hard to know what's best when you are not there with your aging parent. As my mom's caregiver, I tried to keep in mind that my goal was to do what was best for her. I hoped that if my mom had a really strong support circle around her (her children), moving out of her home might not be as devastating. I also wanted my mom to be able to see her children regularly.

I knew moving her into a different setting would be a challenge; therefore, I did not change or make any final decisions on her doctors or other specialty care providers until I knew for sure that she was comfortable with the new situation. My mom and I travelled back to her home in South Carolina every month or two so that she could feel comfortable knowing that her home was still intact.

Having my mom nearby made caregiving easier...and if your parent has any of the s e v e n stages of dementia, they will need increasing support and advocacy from you, your siblings, or other family members. My seventy-plus-year-old mom was diagnosed with dementia several years prior to her showing symptoms. Although this was a very tricky issue, I would offer to help her with certain tasks. I made sure she knew that I was not trying to take over; I was just trying to help. Assuring my mom that I was only there to support helped her transition. As aging parents begin to need assistance with their financial matters, they sometimes question their own dignity and whether or not they can handle their financial matters. Gradually, I assumed total responsibility for balancing my mom's checkbook and all of her bills.

If you have young kids and your parent has been diagnosed with dementia, you need to prepare your kids for the changes. It can be confusing for children to see a grandparent with progressing dementia. It's a good idea to talk to your kids about what dementia is—changes in the brain. Explain that the changes in Grandma are the disease, not her. She is still the person they knew, just different now. Talk with your kids about specific things that may happen and how they may react. For example, if Grandma asks them the same question over and over, help them practice smiling and not correct her. Try to help them feel comfortable and also give them activity ideas to do with her that will keep her busy and keep them interacting. Role-playing is a plus with kids—and remember to encourage them to keep their sense of humor and love. Your local Alzheimer's Association may have good resources for kids.

An Organized Caregiver's Documents List

Being organized can really make life easier for a caregiver. Having information and important documents available when they are needed can sometimes be a challenge for caregivers. Studies show that being organized is a key ingredient to being a successful caregiver (http://www.caregiverslibrary.org). I recommend gathering and placing your loved one's important documents and information in a locked cabinet where they can be obtained quickly. The following **critical documents** are needed to help you stay organized and allow you to access information quickly:

❖ Addresses and phone numbers.

❖ Driver's license or state ID

cards (if your loved one isn't driving, get them a state-issued ID card; in most states they are issued by Bureau of Motor Vehicles like a license).

❖ Organ donor wishes and cards.

❖ Social Security numbers.

❖ Citizenship papers and passport if your loved one is a naturalized citizen or not a U.S. citizen.

❖ Marriage and divorce papers you may need these for insurance, benefits applications, etc.

❖ Military records—there are

several reasons you may need these, including veterans benefits applications and burial arrangements.

❖ End-of-life instructions, including body donor wishes, burial or cremation plans, location, prepaid funeral plans, mortuary, and wishes for services.

❖ At least two emergency contact persons, including the order in which people should be contacted. You may want to create a phone tree so only one person need be called and they call the

next person on the list.

Then collect the minimum

health information you'll need,

including:

- All your loved one's doctors
  and pharmacies (both local
  and mail-order).

- All *medications* and

  supplements, including the

  purpose, dosage, schedule,

  and prescribing doctor.

  Make sure you note any side

effects or reactions to drugs.

- A basic *medical/ health history*, with past and present conditions, blood type, drug allergies, surgeries, and hospitalizations.

- Copies of all *health insurance* cards (including Medicare or Medicaid), phone numbers, websites, and login and password information.

- Health POA, if applicable.

Collect their **legal documents**, including:

- <u>Advanced Directives</u>—including living will and healthcare power of attorney. These may be very long documents, so you can try keeping a copy on a thumb drive to carry with you to the hospital or doctor's appointments.

- A <u>Will or Trust</u>—these also may be very long, but know where they are and remember

that your loved one's attorney
should always be able to send
a copy to anyone who needs it.
Caregivers should also collect all
pertinent **financial information**,
including:

✓ Power of Attorney—
documenting your ability to
manage financial matters.

- ✓ Bank account locations, numbers, and access information: login, password, personal ID number (PIN). Is your name on their account?
- ✓ Safety deposit box location, permission to access, and keys.
- ✓ Credit card numbers, websites, phone numbers, PIN, login, and password information.
- ✓ Property and mortgage documents, website, login, password, automatic payment information.
- ✓ Any other loan documents,

such as a home equity line of credit or a personal loan.

✓ Automobile information, including license and registration number, insurance information, loan information, and roadside assistance plan.

✓ Insurance policies (such as life, disability, health, long-term care, home and auto), including coverage, websites, phone numbers, login, and password information.

Caregivers should make sure they keep all documents and information updated and in a place where they can be easily accessed. Caregivers should make duplicate copies of each document and store the duplicates on a computer, thumb drive, cell phone, or any storage device so that the caregiver and other family members or people with a need to know are aware of where these documents are stored for emergency purposes and as backup copies, if needed.

Chapter 11

Ten Drugs that May Cause Memory Loss

For a long time, doctors dismissed forgetfulness and mental confusion as a normal part of aging. But scientists now know that *memory loss* as you get older is by no means inevitable.

Indeed, the brain can grow new brain cells and reshape their connections throughout life. Most people are familiar with at least some of the things that can impair memory, including alcohol and drug abuse, heavy cigarette smoking, head injuries, stroke, sleep deprivation, severe stress, vitamin B12 deficiency, and illnesses, such as Alzheimer's disease and depression. What many people don't realize is that many commonly prescribed drugs can also interfere with memory. The following chart outlines the top ten types of drug offenders that may cause memory loss. Please consult with your doctor

concerning the risks as well as

alternative treatments available.

Dr. Gybrilla Ballard-Blakes

Information that appears below is adapted from *Women's Brain Health*:

Drug Categories and Examples

1: Anti-anxiety Drugs (Benzodiazepines)
-Alprazolam (Xanax), chlordiazepoxide (Librium), clonazepam (Klonopin), diazepam (Valium), flurazepam (Dalmane), lorazepam (Ativan), midazolam (Versed), quazepam (Doral), temazepam (Restoril), and triazolam (Halcion

2: Cholesterol Drugs (Statins) -
Atorvastatin (Lipitor), fluvastatin (Lescol), lovastatin Mevacor), pravastatin (Pravachol), rosuvastatin (Crestor), and simvastatin (Zocor)

3: Antiseizure Drugs- Acetazolamide (Diamox), carbamazepine (Tegretol), ezogabine (Potiga), gabapentin (Neurontin), lamotrigine (Lamictal), levetiracetam (Keppra), oxcarbazepine (Trileptal), pregabalin (Lyrica), rufinamide (Banzel), topiramate (Topamax), valproic

acid(Depakote), and zonisamide
(Zonegran)

**4: Antidepressant drugs (Tricyclic
antidepressants)-** Amitriptyline (Elavil),
clomipramine(Anafranil), desipramine
(Norpramin), doxepin(Sinequan),
imipramine(Tofranil), nortriptyline
(Pamelor), protriptyline(Vivactil),and
trimipramine (Surmontil)

5: Narcotic painkillers- Fentanyl
(Duragesic), hydrocodone(Norco,
Vicodin),hydromorphone (Dilaudid,
Exalgo), morphine(Astramorph, Avinza),
and oxycodone (OxyContin,Percocet)
{these drugs come in many different
forms, including tablets, solutions for
injection, transdermal patches}.

**6: Parkinson's drugs (Dopamine
agonists)-** Apomorphine (Apokyn),
pramipexole (Mirapex),and ropinirole

7: Hypertension drugs (Beta-blockers)-
Atenolol (Tenormin), carvedilol(Coreg),
metoprolol(Lopressor, Toprol),
propranolol (Inderal),sotalol (Betapace),
timolol Timoptic) and some other drugs
whose chemical names end with "-olol."

8: Sleeping aids- Eszopiclone (Lunesta), zaleplon (Sonata)

9: Incontinence drugs (Antic holinergics)- Darifenacin (Enablex), mirabegron (Myrbetriq), oxybutynin (Ditropan XL, Gelnique, Oxytrol), solifenacin (Vesicare), tolterodine (Detrol) and trospium (Sanctura). Another oxybutynin product, Oxytrol for Women, is sold over the counter.

10: Antihistamines (First generation)- Brompheniramine (Dimetane), carbinoxamine (Clistin), chlorpheniramine (Chlor-Trimeton), clemastine (Tavist), diphenhydramine (Benadryl) and hydroxyzine (Vistaril)

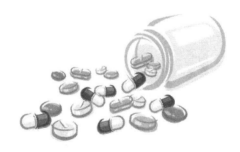

Chapter 12

Dementia Symptom Management Tips

Providing care and activities for the elderly parent isn't always easy, especially when that parent is suffering from some sort of dementia or Alzheimer's (or any condition that causes deterioration of mental function). Learning how to (1) identify behavior issues, (2) understand them, and (3) deal with them in a calm and soothing manner will help to prevent or defuse escalating behaviors that can affect not only the individual, but also the entire family support system.

Identifying a Behavior Issue

The first thing to realize for any caregiver or family member of an elderly parent who has been diagnosed with dementia is that the person suffering from the disorder is not deliberately trying to make your life miserable. Engaging such individuals may seem like an insurmountable chore, and one that nearly always ends in frustration, but this doesn't have to be the case.

First, let's explore some behavior issues that can be associated with activities for the elderly and group efforts:

o Disruptive behavior (shouting, crying, scratching, hitting, etc.)
o Roaming/Wandering
o Aggression
o Combativeness

Three key factors will help a caregiver identify a behavioral issue:

1. Can you see the behavior?
2. Can you rate or measure the

behavior (i.e., mild, moderate, severe)?
3. Can others see the behavior?

Remember that every behavior has a cause: something exists or happened to set the behavior in motion. To put it simply, the wrong button was pushed. In order to prevent that behavior from happening again, caregivers will need to learn to identify which buttons or triggers tend to set an elderly parent off. Here are some ways to help a caregiver find out what such buttons or triggers are:

○ Who was around when the behavior occurred?

- ○ What happened just before the behavior occurred?
- ○ Was the behavior caused by a task that proved too difficult?

The best way to deal with behavior issues is to adapt. Caregivers need to be constantly aware of the signals their elderly parent is giving off and be able to adapt, distract, or steer the parent away from situations that may provoke behavior issues.

Diagnosed with Dementia

It is especially important to engage our parents in social or elderly group functions as much as possible, even if they are suffering from some form of dementia. Remember that there are many different forms and stages of dementia, so you will more than likely have to adapt to various capabilities and factors, such as:

- ➤ Shorter attention spans
- ➤ Inability to stay on task for a given amount of time
- ➤ Unwillingness to participate

`When choosing for your elderly parent, consider focusing on issues that stimulate each of the five senses. Choose something that you know your parent enjoyed in the past. This could be gardening, painting, music, or game playing.

Elderly Activities: Crafts and Games

Here are a few more things to remember:

- ➤ Use skills your parent still has
- ➤ Keep activities short

> ➤ Try to engage communication skills— talk to your elderly parent
> ➤ Try to facilitate motor skills

One idea might be allowing your parent to help fold the laundry (no matter if you have to do it over again!) or encouraging them to paint. Recreational ideas for the elderly parent might also involve outings to the park or the zoo, picking fruit in a nearby orchard, or visiting other friends and family members.

Going anywhere with your parent is important and helps them to stay in touch with the outside world. Try not to isolate your parent. Watch them carefully for signs that they are growing overstimulated, and then distract or guide them to something else or allow them to rest in a quiet area. Activities such as flower arranging, stringing beads, or creating holiday cards may keep your elderly parent engaged and occupied for hours, or they may want to skip from one project to another every few minutes. These types of projects for the elderly help maintain small motor skills and hand-eye coordination, so encourage them as much as possible.

Elderly Music for the Soul

Even though a parent may be suffering from Alzheimer's or another form of dementia, music has a way of soothing the troubled spirit. If your father was especially fond of Glen Miller, play some Glen Miller for him on a CD player in his room. If your mother was smitten with Frank Sinatra, by all means, play Frank for her. Music, such as these examples, can help! Taking special care to supply an aging parent with items such as music may also be a means to help distract or diffuse behavior issues.

Studies have shown that many elders suffering from various stages of dementia showed a decrease in behaviors when exposed to music, television programs, or movies that were popular when they were younger. Remember, identifying triggers and adapting the environment or situation will help you keep your elderly parent engaged and focused, and that will help enhance their quality of life.

Elderly Parents Caregiver Stress:
Ten Steps for Relief

Caregiving is an extremely stressful task—mentally, physically and emotionally.

Caregivers are generally on call 24/7, with very little help from other family members. Caregiving can be demanding, draining, and frustrating task that may take its toll on health, spirit, and psyche.

Caregiver Stress

Today, nearly 80 percent of individuals diagnosed with dementia or various stages of Alzheimer's are cared for at home by adult children or other close family members. In such situations, the caregiver is at an increased risk of stress (http://www.caregiverslibrary.org).

Most caregivers, regardless of the age or needs of an elderly parent, go through periods of stress and anxiety. Caregivers must also take care of family responsibilities as well as the needs of the aging parent, communicating with doctors, dealing with appointments, and handling emotional issues caused by dementia or Alzheimer's.

If you are a caregiver, answer the

following questions to determine if you might be under some level of stress:

- ❖ Question 1: Do you feel that you spend so much time caring for your elderly parent that you don't have any time left over for yourself?

- ❖ Question 2: Do you feel your health has been compromised because of the physical, emotional, or mental demands of caregiving?

- ❖ Question 3: Do you sometimes wish you could leave the care of your elderly parents to someone else?

❖ Question 4: Do you wonder what the future holds for the both of you?

Caregiver Stress: Common Health Problems

Many caregivers suffer from health problems related to stress, including but not limited to:

❖ Depression

❖ Anxiety

❖ Physical injury

❖ Increased risk of drug or alcohol abuse

❖ Decreased immune system functions and

more illnesses

❖ Higher mortality risk

Take into consideration the fact that a caregiver may be required to spend an average of seventy hours of care every week on an elderly parent who has been diagnosed with moderate to severe stages of Alzheimer's. For such reasons, it is vital that caregivers do not neglect their own physical, mental, or emotional health.

Stress Relief for Caregivers of Elderly Parents

Caregivers who practice stress relief measures and try to stay as active as possible feel better about their situation—and themselves—than those who don't. Taking care of the caregivers should be a major priority of family members and friends of those who take care of seniors.

Caregivers themselves can take charge of their health by following a few guidelines for relief every day. Here are ten ways to nurture your own body, spirit and soul, even if you are taking care of a senior twenty-four hours a day:

1. *Take time for yourself*—Even if it's five minutes at a time, try to find a few minutes for

you every day. Go outside. Sit down and meditate. Watch TV. Read a magazine. Just take five-minute increments for yourself as often as possible throughout the day.

2. *Exercise*— fifteen minutes of stretching, dancing...anything to help your body and spirit de-stress.

3. *Get outside*—Every day, try to go outside, even if it's for a

few minutes. Open the windows: a breath of fresh air can be invigorating!

4. *Eat well*—Eat well-balanced and nutritious meals, remember your vitamins, and drink at least sixty-eight ounces of water every day.

5. *Sleep*—This is a tough one, but do try to get at least six to eight hours of sleep every night. If you have to, schedule naps when your elderly parent naps to make up for lost hours.

6. *Smile*—Try to find something

to smile or laugh about every day.

7. *Listen to your body*—Don't ignore your aching back or your growing depression. Listen to your body and take care of it.

8. *Ask for help*—Don't be afraid to ask for help. Many people are more than willing to help but are afraid to butt in or imply that you can't do it yourself.

9. *Zone out*—Read, meditate, pray. Do something that brings you comfort and relief,

and do it every day, without fail.

10. *Set limitations*— Don't push your body to the limit. If something's wrong, get it taken care of before it becomes much worse.

Nurture the Elderly Parent Caregivers

Taking care of an aging parent may offer a sense of accomplishment and pride, but it also takes its toll in obvious and not-so-obvious ways. If you are a caregiver, find community resources to help. There are also adult daycare centers in most states that can give elderly people options to socialize and participate in other activities during the day. If you are the relative of a caregiver, do what you can to make their life easier.

Chapter 13

Thirteen Resources Every Caregiver Should Know About

Here's a list of key resources to help you in your caregiving role. AARP suggests that caregivers should keep this list handy:

Alzheimer's Association
www.alz.org
800-272-3900

Information and support for people
with Alzheimer's disease and their
caregivers.
Operates a 24/7 helpline and care
navigator tools.

Alzheimers.gov
www.alzheimers.gov

The government's free information
resource about Alzheimer's disease
and related dementias.

ARCH Respite Network
www.archrespite.org

Programs and services to allow
caregivers to get a break from
caring for a loved one.

Brighthub
http://www.brighthub.com

How to manage someone else's
money, write wills, and find insurance

information.

Eldercare Locator
www.eldercare.gov
800-677-1116

Connects caregivers to local services
and resources for older adults and
adults with disabilities across the
United States.

Family Caregiver Alliance
www.caregiver.org
800-445-8106

Information, education and services
for family caregivers, including the
Family Care Navigator, a state-by-state
list of services and assistance.

Maryland Department of Aging
www.aging.maryland.gov
410-767-1100

The Maryland Department of Aging
(MDoA) and the statewide network
of 19 Area Agencies on Aging
assist older Marylanders with a
range of services and sources of
information.

Medicare
www.medicare.gov/caregivers
800-Medicare

Provides information about the parts
of Medicare, what's new, and how to
find Medicare plans, facilities, or
providers.

National Alliance for Caregiving
www.caregiving.org

A coalition of national organizations
focused on family caregiving issues.

National Family Caregivers Association
www.caregiveraction.org

Information and education for family
caregivers. Includes the Caregiver
Community Action Network, a
volunteer support network in over
forty states.

The National Clearinghouse for Long-term Care Information
www.longtermcare.gov

Information and tools to plan for future long-term care needs.

Social Security Administration
www.socialsecurity.gov
800-772-1213

Information on retirement and disability benefits, including how to sign up.

State Health Insurance Assistance Program
www.shiptalk.org

A program that offers one-on-one insurance counseling and assistance to people with
Medicare and their families.

Veterans Administration
www.caregiver.va.gov
855-260-3274

Support and services for families caring for veterans. Maintains a Veterans Administration caregiver support line.

References

AARP (2013). Home Health. Retrieved July 3, 2013, from http://www.aarphealthcare.com/choosing-caregiving/aarp-home-health-care.html.

AARP (2013). Legal and Financial Matters. Financial Power of Attorney. Retrieved July 3, 2013, from http://www.aarp.org/relationships/caregiving- resource-center/info-11-2010/lfm_financial_power_of_attorney.html

Aging Care (2013). Connecting Caregivers. Retrieved July 3, 2013, from http://www.agingcare.com

2012 Alzheimer's Disease Facts and Figures confirmed. Retrieved July 12, 2013, from http://www.alz.org/downloads/facts_figures_2012.pdf

Cosmato, Donna and Scheid, Jean. (2011). Steps to Manage an Elderly's Finances Legally. Retrieved July 12, 2013, from http://www.brighthub.com/money/personal-finance/articles/70944.aspx

Healy, Melissa et al. (2012). Tread carefully when talking about lifestyle changes to elderly parents. Retrieved July 6, 2013, from **http://www.betterliving.com**

Stanford University's Study (2005). Risk on Caregivers. Retrieved July 13, 2013, from https://caregiver.org/caregiver-health

Women's Brain Health. Retrieved July 3, 2013, from http://womensbrainhealth.org

Dr. Gybrilla Ballard-Blakes

Dr. Ballard-Blakes is a full adjunct professor for Webster University. She previously held the position of the chief of the personnel security section for the Executive Office for the US Attorney. Dr. Ballard-Blakes acts as a guest speaker for the Federal Government Oversight Managers' courses and Administrator Officers' conferences. She has acted as a guest speaker at several US Attorneys' conferences. Dr. Ballard-Blakes also acts as a personnel security adjudication expert for all US FDIC field offices and has acted as a personnel security adjudication expert for the ninety-four US Attorneys' offices.

Dr. Ballard-Blakes participated in the Joint Security Task Force Center/Personnel Security Research Center (JSTC/PERSEREC) Personnel Security initiative, the US Office of Personnel Management Suitability Working Group,